SPONGE CAKES

Sponge
cakes

WENDY SWEETSER

JOHN BEAUFOY PUBLISHING

First published in the United Kingdom in 2011 by John Beaufoy Publishing,
11 Blenheim Court, 316 Woodstock Road, Oxford OX2 7NS, England
www.johnbeaufoy.com

10 9 8 7 6 5 4 3 2 1

ISBN 978-1-906780-48-7

Project manager: Rosemary Wilkinson
Design: Roger Hammond at bluegum
Photography: Ian Garlick
Illustration: Stephen Dew

Printed in India by Replika Press Pvt Ltd.

RECIPE NOTES

✍ Where milk is used in a recipe,
this can be full-fat, semi-skimmed or
skimmed.

✍ All spoon measurements are level.

✍ Metric and imperial
measurements are not always exact
equivalents, so only follow one set of
measurements within each recipe.

✍ As individual ovens vary, the
cooking times given should only be
taken as a guide. Bake for at least
3/4 of the suggested cooking time
before opening the oven door and
testing to see if the cake is ready.

✍ Oven temperatures have been
given for conventional electric and
gas ovens. For fan ovens, use the
following equivalents:

Electricity °C	Electricity (fan) °C
110	90
120	100
130	110
140	120
150	130
160	140
170	150
180	160
190	170
200	180
220	200

Contents

Getting started

Cakes are a great treat whether we're making a special gâteau for a family birthday or just a simple sponge to share with friends over a cup of coffee or tea. And, whilst supermarkets and bakers offer shelves of ready-made sponges to save us time and trouble, nothing can quite compare with the cake we've lovingly mixed and baked ourselves.

Cake tins

When buying cake tins, it's a case of you get what you pay for. Heavy, solid tins will last a lifetime, thin ones can warp, lose their shape and will not conduct heat evenly when in the oven. It's also important to use the correct size of tin for a recipe. Too shallow a tin and the mix can overflow as it rises, too large a tin and the end result will look flat and anaemic.

Unless a shallower tin is specified in the recipe, a standard cake tin needs to be 6–7 cm/2½–3 in deep. Although individual recipes will vary, when substituting a ring tin for a round or square tin, subtract about 10 minutes from the cooking time and vice versa.

Fixed-base, loose-bottomed and spring-clip tins are interchangeable in most recipes. However, a delicate cake or one with a topping that could be damaged if the cake is turned upside down onto a cooling rack, is best baked in a loose-bottomed or spring-clip tin. Drizzle cakes, where a syrup is poured over a hot cake straight from the oven, are best baked in tins with a fixed base.

Although lots of different tins have been used to bake the cakes in this book, it's not necessary to buy every one – unless of course you're a really keen baker with lots of space! Where ring or bundt tins are used, the capacity of the tin has been included in the recipe so a tin of a similar size can be substituted. For a DIY ring tin, place a clean, empty food can in the centre of a round tin. Weight the tin with baking beans to prevent it from being pushed over as the cake mixture rises.

Silicone moulds and non-stick tins

Although silicone moulds and tins coated with a non-stick surface might seem the answer to a novice baker's prayers, both can have their disadvantages.

Silicone moulds are unstable and bendy so removing a sponge without cracking it can be difficult, also during baking a cake may not brown as much as in a traditional tin. Cheaper moulds can produce an unpleasant smell that permeates the cake, they won't distribute heat evenly and some mixtures will stick despite manufacturers' claims to the contrary, so the base and sides will still need greasing.

Non-stick tins are easy to clean but their non-stick properties can't always be relied on especially when a tin has been well used. Tins with a black non-stick coating conduct heat more evenly than other coatings.

Ways of making sponge cakes

Creamed method: butter and sugar are beaten together until light and creamy. Eggs are then added gradually with a little of the flour to prevent the mix from curdling, before the remaining flour and other ingredients are folded in.

Whisked method: eggs and sugar are whisked for several minutes until they have a mousse-like consistency before flour, melted butter and other ingredients are gently folded in so that the mixture doesn't lose the air that has been whisked in. An electric whisk saves time and takes the effort out of making this type of cake and a large metal spoon is best for folding ingredients together. When the mix has been poured into the tin, tap the tin lightly on the work surface so any large air bubbles trapped in the mixture rise to the surface and burst.

All-in-one method: all the ingredients are placed together in a mixing bowl and whisked or beaten until evenly combined.

Techniques

Lining tin: brush the base and/or sides of the tin with a mild-flavoured oil, such as sunflower, and line with non-stick baking parchment cut to fit.

To prepare a tin that can't be lined with baking parchment, such as a ring or bundt tin, brush the inside of the tin with oil and dust with flour, shaking out any excess before spooning in the cake mixture. If the tin is elaborately shaped, it's worth buying a product such as Cake Release (available from cook shops or from the internet) to grease the tin, so the cake turns out easily.

Smoothing mixture level in tin: a runny cake mix will find its own level in a tin but for thicker mixtures, spread level with a palette knife to ensure an even rise.

Testing for done-ness: very light mixtures, such as those for Swiss rolls and whisked sponges, are ready when they feel springy to the touch and begin to shrink from the sides of the tin. For heavier mixtures, the most reliable method is to push a

skewer into the centre of the cake and check that it comes out clean. If not, return the cake to the oven for 5-10 minutes and test again.

Turning out onto a wire rack: a cake will cool more quickly if it is turned out onto a wire rack. When the cake comes out of the oven, leave it in the tin to firm up for about 5 minutes – delicate cakes are best left a little longer – then turn out upside-down onto a wire rack and peel off any lining paper. Note that cooking times don't include time needed for the cake to cool.

Spreading frosting: use a palette knife to spread frosting evenly over a cake. Use a semi-circular motion, smoothing it over the top and sides.

Flours and raising agents

The recipes use plain flour and either baking powder or bicarbonate of soda (or both) as a raising agent. If self-raising flour is available, this can be substituted – use the same quantity as given for plain flour and omit the raising agent.

Bicarbonate of soda is four times as strong as baking powder so needs to be used sparingly. In order for it to work it needs to combine with an acid, such as fruit or buttermilk.

For those who are intolerant to wheat or gluten, polenta, rice flour, ground almonds or potato flour combined with gluten-free baking powder can be used instead of wheat flour.

What went wrong?

It is important to measure ingredients carefully using scales and a proper set of measuring spoons, the tin should be the correct size and the cake tested to ensure it's cooked before being removed from the oven.

Other things to watch out for are:

✍ **Top badly cracked or peaked too much:** Too much raising agent. Too much mixture in tin. Oven too hot.

✍ **Top sunk in the middle:** Too much raising agent. Mixture too wet. Tin too small.

✍ **Overbrowning or hard crust:** Oven too hot. Over-baking.

✍ **Cake forms a crusty ring round the sides:** Tin over-greased.

✍ **Speckling on top:** Insufficient creaming so sugar not dissolved.

✍ **Rubbery texture:** Too much egg or milk. Flour beaten in rather than folded or stirred in.

✍ **Dry, crumbly texture:** Mixture too dry. Fat and sugar not creamed properly. Too much raising agent. Baked too slowly.

Keeping sponge cakes

Unlike fruit cakes, sponges don't improve the longer you keep them, so serve them as soon as possible after baking.

Fat-free sponges dry out quickly and are best eaten on the day they are made but cakes that contain butter or another fat will keep well in an airtight tin for several days. Any cake with fresh cream or cream cheese in the filling or frosting needs to be stored in the fridge. Plain sponges can be made ahead and frozen. Defrost and decorate them when ready to serve.

Icings, frostings and fillings

Mix and match these according to personal taste with those suggested in the individual cake recipes. Quantities of each are enough for an average size cake.

Glacé icing

This simple icing has a sweet taste that can be sharpened with a little orange or lemon zest and juice.

225 g/8 oz icing sugar
3–4 tbsp water

Sieve the icing sugar into a bowl and stir in enough water to give a smooth icing that will coat the back of the spoon in a thick layer. A few drops of vanilla, almond or peppermint flavouring, food colouring or fruit syrups, such as grenadine, can also be stirred in. Use immediately as the icing will quickly form a crust.

Flavoured glacé icings:

Citrus: replace the water with fresh lemon, orange or lime juice
Chocolate: replace 1 tablespoon of the icing sugar with cocoa powder
Coffee: replace the water with cold strong black coffee
Grown-up: replace the water with rum, brandy, Tia Maria, orange Curaçao, limoncello or similar

Buttercream

Creamy and sweet, the proportion of sugar to butter can be varied according to personal taste.

175 g /6 oz unsalted butter, softened
225 g/8 oz icing sugar
1 tbsp milk

Beat the butter in a bowl until creamy. Sieve in the icing sugar, a little at a time, beating well after each addition. Stir in the milk to soften. A few drops of food colouring can also be added. Use immediately or press cling film over the surface to prevent a crust from forming and keep refrigerated.

Flavoured buttercreams:

Coffee: stir in 1 tbsp cold strong black coffee
Vanilla: stir in 1 tsp vanilla essence
Orange/Lemon: beat in the grated zest of 1 small orange or 1 lemon

Marshmallow frosting

A sweet, foamy favourite. Best used on a plain cake that is not too sweet.

275 g/10 oz granulated sugar
2 large egg whites
4 tbsp cold water
1 tbsp light corn syrup or runny honey
¼ tsp cream of tartar

Whisk all the ingredients together in a large heatproof bowl until the sugar dissolves. Stand the bowl over a pan of simmering water (without letting the bottom of the bowl touch the water) and, using an electric hand whisk, beat on medium speed until fluffy – this will take about 4 minutes. Turn up the speed to high and continue to whisk until very thick – about 3 minutes. Remove the bowl to the work surface and keep whisking until the base of it is cold. Use immediately.

Chocolate icing

Rich and smooth, its level of sweetness depends on the type of chocolate used. Use dark chocolate with no more than 70% cocoa solids or it will be too bitter. Use milk chocolate with at least 30% cocoa solids and use the best quality white chocolate you can find.

225 g/8 oz dark, milk or white chocolate, chopped
75 g/3 oz unsalted butter

Melt the chocolate and butter together in a bowl over a pan of simmering water, stirring until smooth. Use immediately.

Chocolate ganache

Lighter and creamier than chocolate icing, again its sweetness level depends on the chocolate used. See 'Chocolate Icing' for information on the type of chocolate to use for best results.

175 ml/6 fl oz double cream or full-fat crème fraîche
250 g/9 oz dark, milk or white chocolate, chopped

Bring the cream to the boil in a small pan, remove from the heat and stir in the chocolate. Leave until the chocolate has melted, then beat with a wooden spoon until smooth. Leave to cool at room temperature, not in the fridge, until thick enough to spread, stirring occasionally, then whisk for 1-2 minutes until light. If the icing becomes too thick, microwave on medium power in 15 second bursts until it returns to the right consistency.

Cream cheese frosting

115 g/4 oz full-fat cream cheese
50 g/2 oz unsalted butter, softened
225 g/8 oz icing sugar

Whisk together the cream cheese, butter and icing sugar until smooth and creamy. Use immediately, or press cling film over the surface to prevent a crust forming and keep refrigerated.

Fruits, jam and cream

Sponge layers can be sandwiched together with jam and topped with whipped double cream. Fresh berries or chopped fruit, such as mangoes, peaches, nectarines, pineapple and apricots can be added instead of or in addition to the jam. Choose a red jam such as raspberry or strawberry for berries and apricot or peach jam for orange fruits.

I

Snowtrip planner

We have teamed up with Igluski.com to give you a simple guide to planning the perfect ski holiday. Igluski.com is the largest independent retailer of ski holidays in the UK. It is the one stop shop for all your ski and snowboard holiday needs in France and the French Alps.

Here are the 5 main tips to enable you to make the right holiday or trip decision:

1. Choose the resort

Whether you're a seasoned expert, a total beginner, or more interested in the après ski than skiing itself there is a resort to suit your needs. Experts will be impressed by Chamonix's extensive ski range, whilst beginners will enjoy learning on the gentle slopes of La Plagne. Val D'Isère is renowned for its après ski, whereas the tranquil and friendly resort of Flaine is ideal for families.

2. Get to know your resort

No more need to spend your first day searching for the ski lifts, or only discovering that perfect après ski hangout on the last day. Webcams, resort maps and virtual tours will make you feel right at home as soon as you get there.

3. Plan your descent

Use Snowfinder Piste Maps or Igluski.com piste maps to allow you to explore the mountain before you even hit the slopes. Plan where you want to go now and spend less time on the side of runs, piste map in hand.

4. Watch the snowfall

Keep up to date with the latest snow news with regular snow reports. Archives also allow you to research the previous year's snow fall whetting your appetite for the season to come.

5. Go prepared

Make sure you have all the equipment, insurance and knowledge you need to make your trip perfect.

www.snowfinder.co.uk

Accommodation

Getting to the slopes is easier and more affordable than ever before.

The choice of accommodation and travel options for a winter sports holiday is ever increasing. You can stay in a cosy chalet, luxury hotel or budget apartment, you can fly, drive or take the train, and you can go for a short break as well as the traditional week long holiday.

Researching and booking your holiday is also easier than ever before with the help of specialist winter sports travel retailer **Igluski**, who have done all the hard work for you and collated all the accommodation and travel options for you on their website **www.igluski.com**, creating a one-stop-shop complete with snow reports, webcams and weather forecasts to help plan your trip.

A ski holiday package which includes your accommodation, resort transfers and flights is still the best value means of getting on the piste – self-catering packages start from as little as **£200 per person**!

A chalet holiday typically includes your breakfast, afternoon tea and three course evening meals with wine and chalet packages start from just **£400**, group discounts of up to 1 in 4 go free are also available on chalet holidays.

When booking a package through a specialist, such as **Igluski**, you can also find excellent lift pass and equipment hire savings that would not be available when you get to your resort.

To plan your ski holiday and see all the latest offers and savings visit
www.igluski.com
or call on **020 8544 6639**
to discuss your requirements.

www.natives.co.uk

Fly-on-the-wall documentaries would like you to believe it's a shagfest for young hedonists escaping reality. Hey, we're not denying that is part of it, but the reality is that if you're expecting an easy life you're in for a shock.

There are a number of key things you need to know/think about, so we've asked *Natives* to list them for us and make it easy for you:

1. Getting a job

Either you know someone out there, you get a job with a tour operator, chalet, bar firm in London! or do it properly and get on one of the *Natives* courses run in London! These cover: available jobs and the required skills and experiences; the package and possible 'extras' you can expect; application forms and CVs; interview advice and tips - you've got there, so get it right; and the questions should you be asking a potential employer.

If you are planning to look for more than just odd jobs during the season, then have a look at the *Natives Ski Jobs* service first. Competition for jobs from other 'skibums' can be very tough (esp in the most popular resorts - *Val d'Isère, Méribel/Mottaret and Chamonix*).

It can take weeks, or longer, to find work when you arrive, so to help out, why not visit the website and search through the database of companies recruiting for this winter to find the job you're looking for. There can be hundreds of jobs listed here, so know what you want to work in, read the job descriptions and requirements, ensure that your skills and experiences match the job requirements and get applying. Good luck!

Applications are processed between July and October for the following season.

2. Job types

These include: ski guides; chalet staff; resort reps & managers; club hotel managers; chefs; plongeurs; bar staff; nannies; maintenance workers; and various peak season jobs. For more details on what these entail, check out the website.

3. Accomodation

You can pretty much guarantee that whoever you work for, unless you're a senior rep or very lucky that you'll have to share. So valued are single rooms that a loft or a dank dungeon is viewed with respect.

Maybe you want to go out for the season and look for part time work when you get there? Or maybe you've lined up a job with a local company and need to sort out your own accomodation? *Natives* can help: individuals, couples or groups looking for their own accomodation; or, individuals or couples looking to share accomodation. They can also match you up with flat mates.

4. Visa requirements

Most of you will be EU passport holders. What this actually means is widely open to debate. Most employers insist that you *must* have an EU passport (to work in Europe). However this can vary by country and resort within a country. And indeed many employers have set up their businesses so that they can legally employ anyone with a UK working visa and NI number.

You may also have *Ancestry Visas, Right of Abode, UK Working Visas* These are not normally sufficient to work in EU countries. *Ancestry visas,* right of abode and UK working visas do not count as an EU passport.

For the French Embassy, check out the following website:
http://www.france.diplomatie.fr/venir/visas

X1 SPORTS INSURANCE

- ● Extreme Sports, Ski & Snowboarding
- ● Off piste as standard
- ● We can cover under 70's

EUROPE
£53*
Annual cover

WORLDWIDE
£77*
Annual cover

Buy online at
www.x1sportsinsurance.com

or call
0870 343 01 38

"Save pounds on your annual ski insurance with X1 Sports"
Graham Bell, British Olympian

family
favourites

Serves 8
Prep time: 25 mins
Cook time: 25–30 mins

225 g/8 oz unsalted butter, softened
225 g/8 oz caster sugar
4 large eggs
225 g/8 oz plain flour
2 tsp baking powder

FILLING
115 g/4 oz mascarpone cheese
100 ml/3½ fl oz double cream
6 tbsp seedless raspberry jam
115 g/4 oz raspberries
icing sugar, to dust

Victoria sandwich

1 Grease and line two 20 cm/8 in sandwich tins, 4 cm/1½ in deep. Preheat the oven to 180°C/350°F/Gas 4.

2 Beat the butter and sugar together until creamy. Beat in the eggs one at a time, adding a tablespoon of the flour with each egg. Sieve in the rest of the flour and baking powder and fold in until evenly combined.

3 Divide the mixture between the cake tins, level and bake for 25–30 minutes or until springy to the touch. Cool in the tins for 5 minutes before turning out onto a wire rack to cool completely. Peel off the paper.

4 For the filling, stir together the mascarpone and cream until smooth and thick enough to spread. Spoon 4 tablespoons of the jam onto one cake and spread in an even layer, followed by the mascarpone cream. Lift the second cake layer on top. Chill until ready to serve.

5 Just before serving, warm the remaining jam and brush it over the top. Cover with raspberries and dust with icing sugar.

Serves 6
Prep time: 30 mins
Cook time: 30–35 mins

175 g/6 oz unsalted butter, softened
175 g/6 oz caster sugar, plus extra
for rolling out marzipan
3 large eggs
175 g/6 oz plain flour

2 tsp baking powder
75 g/3 oz ground rice
grated zest of 1 orange
few drops of orange food colouring
2 tbsp cocoa powder
2 tbsp milk
4 tbsp apricot jam
350 g/12 oz yellow marzipan

Choc-orange battenberg

1 Grease and line a 20 cm/8 in square cake tin and place a folded strip of greased foil down the centre of the tin to divide it in two. Preheat the oven to 180°C/350°F/Gas 4.

2 Beat the butter and sugar together until creamy. Beat in the eggs one at a time, adding a tablespoon of flour with each egg. Sieve in the rest of the flour and baking powder. Fold in with the ground rice. Spoon half the mix into another bowl.

3 Stir the orange zest and a little food colouring into one bowl and the cocoa powder and milk into the other. Spoon the orange mixture into one side of the tin and the cocoa mixture into the other, spreading the tops of both level.

4 Bake for 30–35 minutes until well risen and springy to the touch. Cool in the tin for 5 minutes before turning out onto a wire rack to cool completely. Remove the paper and foil.

5 Cut each cake in half lengthways to give 4 strips. Warm the jam, brush over the sides and layer two on top of the other two, alternating the colours. Brush the outside with jam. Roll out the marzipan thinly on a surface dusted with caster sugar and wrap around the cake. Press it in place and trim the edges.

Serves 8
Prep time: 20 mins
Cook time: 45 mins

150 g/5 oz unsalted butter, softened
175 g/6 oz golden caster sugar
2 large eggs
175 g/6 oz plain flour

2 tsp baking powder
1 tsp ground cinnamon
115 g/4 oz ground almonds
90 g/3½ oz sultanas
75 ml/3 fl oz milk
1–2 dessert apples, such as Granny Smith or Cox
juice of ½ lemon

Danish apple and sultana cake

1 Grease and line a 23 cm/9 in spring-clip tin. Preheat the oven to 190°C/375°F/Gas 5.

2 Beat the butter and 150 g/5 oz of the sugar together until smooth and creamy. Beat in the eggs one at a time, adding a tablespoon of the flour with each egg. Sieve in the rest of the flour, the baking powder and cinnamon. Add the almonds and sultanas and fold everything together until evenly combined. Finally stir in the milk.

3 Spoon the mixture into the tin and spread level. Peel, core and thinly slice the apples. Toss in a bowl with the lemon juice, then scatter over the top of the cake.

4 Dust with the remaining sugar and bake for 45 minutes or until just firm. Cool in the tin for 10 minutes before transferring the cake to a wire rack to cool completely and removing the paper.

Serves 8
Prep time: 30 mins plus chilling
Cook time: 50 mins

3 large eggs
150 ml/5 fl oz sunflower oil
150 g/5 oz thick natural yoghurt
4 tbsp clear honey
75 g/3 oz light muscovado sugar

225 g/8 oz plain flour
2 tsp baking powder
50 g/2 oz cocoa powder

TO DECORATE
1 quantity of chocolate ganache,
see page 13
chocolate shavings

Chocolate yoghurt cake

1 Grease and line a 19 cm/7 in square cake tin. Preheat the oven to 170°C/325°F/Gas 3.

2 In a mixing bowl, beat together the eggs, oil, yoghurt, honey and sugar until combined. Sieve in the flour, baking powder and cocoa powder and fold in using a large metal spoon.

3 Pour into the tin and bake for 50 minutes or until a skewer pushed into the centre comes out clean.

4 Cool in the tin for 10 minutes before turning out onto a wire rack to cool completely. Remove the paper.

5 To decorate, split the cake in half through the centre and sandwich with a little of the ganache. Cover the top and sides with the rest, then gently press over the chocolate shavings and chill for 30 minutes before serving.

TIP
To make the chocolate shavings, drag a vegetable peeler across a bar of firm but not too hard chocolate to shave off flakes and curls.

Serves 8
Prep time: 30 mins
Cook time: 25 mins

175 g/6 oz unsalted butter, softened
175 g/6 oz light muscovado sugar
1 tbsp coffee essence
3 large eggs
225 g/8 oz plain flour

2 tsp baking powder
1 tbsp milk
50 g/2 oz chopped walnuts

TO DECORATE
1 quantity of coffee buttercream, see page 12
walnut halves and chopped walnuts
chocolate coffee beans

Walnut and coffee sponge

1 Grease and line two 20 cm/8 in sandwich tins, 4 cm/1¹/₂ in deep. Preheat the oven to 190°C/375°F/Gas 5.

2 In a mixing bowl, beat the butter with the sugar until creamy. Stir in the coffee essence, then beat in the eggs one at a time, adding a tablespoon of the flour with each egg. Sieve in the rest of the flour and baking powder and fold in. Finally stir in the milk and walnuts.

3 Divide the mixture between the tins and spread level. Bake for 25 minutes or until springy to the touch. Cool in the tins for 5 minutes, then turn out onto a wire rack to cool completely and remove papers.

4 To decorate, sandwich the cake layers with some of the buttercream and spread the rest over the top and sides. Top with walnut halves, a few chopped walnuts and chocolate coffee beans.

Serves 8
Prep time: 30 mins
Cook time: 40–45 mins

3 large eggs
200 g/7 oz caster sugar
grated zest of 1 lemon
50 g/2 oz unsalted butter, melted
and cooled

115 ml/4 fl oz milk
225 g/8 oz plain flour
1 tsp baking powder

TO DECORATE
6 tbsp apricot jam
1 quantity of vanilla buttercream,
see page 12
75 g/3 oz toasted flaked almonds

Lemon layer cake with vanilla frosting

1 Grease and line a 20 cm/8 in round cake tin. Preheat the oven to 180°C/350°F/Gas 4.

2 Put the eggs, caster sugar and lemon zest in a mixing bowl and whisk until thick, creamy and pale-coloured.

3 Drizzle the melted butter around the edge of the bowl and fold in with the milk using a large metal spoon. Once combined, sieve the flour and baking powder over the top and gently fold in until all the ingredients are evenly combined.

4 Pour the mixture into the tin and bake for 40–45 minutes or until a skewer pushed into the centre comes out clean. Leave to cool in the tin for 10 minutes before turning out on a wire rack to cool completely. Remove the paper.

5 To decorate, split the cake horizontally into three layers and sandwich with the apricot jam. Spread the buttercream over the top and sides, rough up with a fork and press the almonds all over. Chill until ready to serve.

Serves 16
Prep time: 20 mins
Cook time: 25–30 mins

125 g/4¹/₂ oz plain flour
375 g/13 oz caster sugar
10 large egg whites

¹/₂ tsp cream of tartar
finely grated zest of 1 lemon
¹/₂ tsp vanilla extract

TO SERVE
icing sugar, to dust
a selection of fresh berries

Angel cake with fresh berries

1 Preheat the oven to 190°C/375°F/Gas 5.

2 Sieve the flour into a bowl and stir in half the sugar. In another large bowl, whisk the egg whites with the cream of tartar until standing in soft peaks. Whisk in the remaining sugar, a little at a time, until the egg whites are stiff.

3 Fold in the lemon zest, vanilla extract and flour mixture using a large metal spoon.

4 Spoon into an ungreased 23 cm/9 in angel cake tin, 10 cm/4 in deep, level and bake for 25–30 minutes or until a skewer pushed into the cake comes out clean.

5 Invert onto a wire rack and leave the cake to cool in the tin before running a knife around the edge to release it. Serve dusted with icing sugar and with a selection of fresh berries.

TIP
The tin should not be greased as this will prevent the cake from rising.

Serves 8
Prep time: 20 mins
Cook time: 12–15 mins

4 large eggs
115 g/4 oz caster sugar, plus extra
to dust
115 g/4 oz plain flour
1 tbsp warm water

FILLING
150 ml/5 fl oz double cream
2 tbsp lemon curd
175 g/6 oz strawberries, hulled and
roughly chopped

Swiss roll with strawberries

1 Grease and line a 33 x 23 cm/13 x 9 in Swiss roll tin.
Preheat the oven to 190°C/375°F/Gas 5.

2 Stand a large mixing bowl over a pan of simmering water,
making sure the bottom doesn't touch the water. Add the eggs
and sugar and whisk until pale and the mixture leaves a thick
trail when the beaters are lifted. Remove the bowl to the work
surface and continue whisking until the base of it feels cool.

3 Fold in the warm water with a large metal spoon, sieve the
flour over the top and gently fold in. Turn the mixture into
the tin, spreading it into the corners and bake for 12–15
minutes or until golden brown and just firm to the touch.

4 Sprinkle a sheet of baking parchment with caster sugar and
turn the cake out onto it. Remove the lining paper. Trim the
edges, then score the cake across 2.5 cm/1 in from one short
side without cutting all the way through. Roll up with the
parchment inside. Lift onto a wire rack and leave to cool.

5 For the filling, whisk the cream and lemon curd together
until thick. When ready to serve, unroll the cake, spread with
the lemon cream and scatter over the strawberries. Re-roll
without the parchment and dust with extra caster sugar.

Serves 8
Prep time: 30 mins
Cook time: 30 mins

175 g/6 oz unsalted butter, softened
115 g/4 oz caster sugar
2 tbsp clear honey
3 large eggs
225 g/ 8 oz plain flour

115 g/4 oz blueberries
2 tsp baking powder
1/2 tsp ground cinnamon

TO DECORATE

1 quantity of glacé icing,
see page 12

a selection of fresh berries and
currants

Iced honey sponge with fruits of the forest

1 Grease a 1.4 l/2¹/₂ pt ring tin and dust with flour. Preheat
the oven to 180°C/350°F/Gas 4.

2 In a mixing bowl, beat the butter and sugar until creamy,
then stir in the honey. Beat in the eggs one at a time, adding
a tablespoon of flour with each egg. Dust the blueberries with
a little of the remaining flour and sieve the rest with the
baking powder and cinnamon into the bowl, then fold in
together with the blueberries.

3 Spoon the mixture into the tin, level and bake for
30 minutes or until a skewer pushed into the cake comes out
clean. Cool in the tin for 10 minutes before turning out onto
a wire rack to cool completely.

4 To decorate, spread the glacé icing over the top of the
cake, letting it run down the sides. Decorate with fresh
berries and currants before the icing sets.

2

let's party

Serves 8–10
Prep time: 1 hour
Cook time: 25–30 mins

CHOCOLATE CAKE
175 g/6 oz unsalted butter, softened
175 g/6 oz light muscovado sugar
3 large eggs
175 g/6 oz plain flour

1 1/2 tbsp cocoa powder
1 1/2 tsp baking powder

TO DECORATE
1 quantity of milk chocolate ganache, see page 13
white and coloured sugarpaste icing or marzipan
small sweets

Toy town train sponge

1 To make the cake, grease and base line two 20 cm/8 in sandwich tins, 4 cm/1 1/2 in deep. Preheat the oven to 180°C/350°F/Gas 4.

2 Beat the butter and sugar together until creamy. Beat in the eggs one at a time, adding a tablespoon of the flour with each egg. Sieve in the rest of the flour, the cocoa powder and baking powder, then fold in.

3 Divide the mixture between the tins and spread level. Bake for 25–30 minutes or until springy to the touch. Cool in the tins for 5 minutes before turning out onto a wire rack to cool completely. Remove the papers.

4 Sandwich the cake layers with some of the ganache and spread the remainder over the top and sides.

5 Cut out shapes from thinly rolled, coloured sugarpaste icing or marzipan for a train engine, wheels and carriages and press in place while the icing is still wet. Top the carriages with sweets for cargo and add clouds of steam cut from white sugarpaste from the engine funnel.

Serves 8–10
Prep time: 45 mins plus setting
Cook time: 40–45 mins

150 g/5 oz dark chocolate, chopped
2 tbsp strong black coffee
115 g/4 oz unsalted butter, softened
115 g/4 oz light muscovado sugar
3 large eggs, separated
65 g/2½ oz plain flour
1 tsp baking powder
65 g/2½ oz potato flour

FILLING AND DECORATION
225 g/8 oz full-fat cream cheese
75 g/3 oz caster sugar
200 g/7 oz white chocolate, chopped
250 ml/9 fl oz double cream
1 tbsp cold strong black coffee
chocolate hearts
cocoa powder, to dust

Mocha chocolate heart

1 Grease and line a heart-shaped tin measuring 20 cm/8 in across its widest part. Preheat the oven to 180°C/350°F/Gas 4.

2 Melt the chocolate with the coffee in a bowl over a pan of simmering water. In another bowl, beat the butter and sugar together until creamy. Beat in the egg yolks and stir in the melted, cooled chocolate.

3 Sieve in the plain flour, baking powder and potato flour, then fold in. Whisk the egg whites until stiff, stir in 1 tablespoon, then fold in the remainder. Spoon into the tin, level and bake for 40–45 minutes or until a skewer pushed into the centre comes out clean. Cool in the tin for 10 minutes, then turn out onto a wire rack to cool. Remove the paper.

4 Whisk the cream cheese and sugar together until smooth. Melt the chocolate, stirring until smooth and add to the cream cheese. Whip, then fold in 150 ml/5 fl oz of the cream. Split the cake in half, then sandwich together with the filling. Chill until firm. Whip the remaining cream and coffee and spread over the top. Decorate with the hearts and dust with cocoa powder.

Serves: about 60
Prep time: 2–2¹/₂ hours plus setting

Cook time: 40–45 mins
(15 cm/6 in cake),
1–1¹/₄ hours (23 cm/9 in) cake),
1¹/₂ hours (30 cm/12 in) cake)

Wedding bells

CAKES

Top tier -15cm/6in:

115 g/4 oz unsalted butter, softened

115 g/4 oz caster sugar

2 large eggs

175 g/6 oz plain flour

1 tsp vanilla essence

1¹/₂ tsp baking powder

1 tbsp milk

Middle tier - 23cm/9in:

225 g/8 oz unsalted butter, softened

225 g/8 oz caster sugar

4 large eggs

350 g/12 oz plain flour

1¹/₂ tsp vanilla essence

1 tbsp baking powder

2¹/₂ tbsp milk

Bottom tier - 30cm/12in:

450 g/1 lb unsalted butter, softened

450 g/1 lb caster sugar

8 large eggs

700 g/1¹/₂ lb plain flour

2¹/₂ tsp vanilla essence

2 tbsp baking powder

5 tbsp milk

TO DECORATE

Top tier: 1 quantity of white chocolate icing, see page 13

Middle tier: 1¹/₂ quantities of white chocolate icing

Bottom tier: 2¹/₂ quantities of white chocolate icing

fresh flowers

butterflies made from edible wafer paper and piped writing icing

1 Grease and line one 15 cm/6 in, one 23 cm/9 in and one 30 cm/12 in deep, round cake tin. Preheat the oven to 180°C/350°F/Gas 4.

2 For each tier, beat the butter and sugar together until creamy. Beat in the eggs one at a time, adding one tablespoon of the flour with each egg. Stir in the vanilla extract. Sieve in the rest of the flour and baking powder and

continued next page

fold in. Finally stir in the milk. Spoon into the tins, level and bake the top tier for 40–45 minutes, the middle for 1–1¼ hours and the bottom for 1½ hours or until a skewer pushed into the centre comes out clean. Cool in the tins for 10 minutes before turning out onto wire racks to cool completely and peeling off the lining papers.

3 To decorate, stand each tier on a wire rack over a plate or baking sheet and pour over the icing, smoothing it over the top and sides with a palette knife. Leave in a cool place until set.

4 To assemble, place the bottom tier on a board or large platter and stack the middle and top tiers on top. Decorate with fresh flowers and edible wafer paper butterflies.

TIPS

To make the butterflies, trace shapes onto edible wafer paper. Cut them out with scissors and fold carefully in half. Open out so they are 'V' shaped, decorate with piped coloured writing icing and leave to set on crumpled cling film.

If transporting the cake, keep the tiers separate and assemble on arrival.

The cakes can be stacked directly on top of each other or the two upper tiers placed on thin cake cards, which will make them easier to separate and cut.

Serves 10–12

Prep time: 30 mins plus soaking

Cook time: 50 mins

275 g/10 oz plain flour

2½ tsp baking powder

175 ml/6 fl oz sunflower oil

175 g/6 oz golden caster sugar

5 large eggs

grated zest of 2 large or 3 small lemons

175 g/6 oz natural Greek yoghurt

SYRUP

115 g/4 oz golden caster sugar

50 ml/2 fl oz water

½ tsp ground cinnamon

grated zest and juice of 1 small orange

Greek Easter cake

1 Grease and flour a 2.4 l/4 pt bundt tin or a round cake tin with a similar capacity. Preheat the oven to 170°C/325°F/Gas 3.

2 Sieve the flour and baking powder into a bowl. Measure the sunflower oil into a jug, then add the sugar, eggs, lemon zest and yoghurt and whisk until mixed. Pour into the dry ingredients and stir until evenly combined.

3 Spoon into the tin and bake for 50 minutes or until a skewer pushed into the cake comes out clean.

4 When the cake is almost cooked, make the syrup. Put the sugar, water and cinnamon into a small pan and heat gently until the sugar dissolves. Bring to the boil and leave to bubble for 2 minutes. Remove from the heat and stir in the orange zest and juice.

5 When the cake is ready, remove from the oven and leave to cool in the tin for 5 minutes. Turn it out onto a cooling rack set over a plate and spoon over half the syrup. Leave for 10 minutes to soak in, then spoon over the rest and leave the cake to cool completely.

Serves 8
Prep time: 45 mins
Cook time: 50 mins

150 g/5 oz unsalted butter
150 g/5 oz caster sugar
1 tsp vanilla essence
4 large eggs, separated
75 g/3 oz plain flour
1 tsp baking powder
115 g/4 oz ground almonds

FROSTING AND DECORATION
1 tbsp maple syrup
50 g/2 oz unsalted butter, cut into small pieces
1 tbsp milk
1/2 tsp vanilla essence
225 g/8 oz icing sugar
stars cut from white sugarpaste icing, made 1 day ahead and left until hard
edible silver paint and edible glitter
ribbon

Starry starry night cake

1 Grease and line a 20 cm/8 in round cake tin. Preheat the oven to 180°C/350°F/Gas 4.

2 Beat the butter and caster sugar together until creamy, then stir in the vanilla and egg yolks. In a separate bowl, whisk the egg whites until standing in soft peaks. Sieve the flour and baking powder into the creamed mixture, then stir in with the almonds. Stir in a spoonful of the whisked egg whites to soften the mixture, then fold in the rest with a large metal spoon.

3 Spoon the mixture into the tin, level and bake for 50 minutes or until a skewer pushed into the centre comes out clean. Cool in the tin for 10 minutes before removing to a wire rack to cool completely and peeling off the paper.

4 For the frosting, melt the maple syrup, butter and milk in a small pan. Stir in the vanilla. Sieve the icing sugar into a bowl, then pour over the syrup mixture, stirring until smooth. Cool, then beat with a wooden spoon until thick enough to spread over the top and sides of the cake. Add stars outlined with silver paint. Dust with glitter and tie a ribbon around the cake.

Serves 10–12
Prep time: 40 mins
Cook time: 1 hour

200 g/7 oz dark chocolate, chopped
200 g/7 oz unsalted butter, cut in small pieces
115 ml/4 fl oz cold black coffee
175 g/6 oz plain flour
1 tsp baking powder
1/2 tsp bicarbonate of soda

115 g/4 oz light muscovado sugar
115 g/4 oz caster sugar
3 large eggs
75 ml/3 fl oz buttermilk

TO DECORATE

1 quantity of marshmallow frosting, see page 12

sugarpaste or marzipan flowers and leaves

sugar sprinkles

Chocolate buttermilk cake

1 Grease a 1.8 l/3 pt ring tin or a round cake tin with a similar capacity. Preheat the oven to 160°C/325°F/Gas 3.

2 Put the chocolate and butter in a pan, add the coffee and heat gently until melted. Stir until smooth.

3 Sieve the flour, baking powder and bicarbonate of soda into a bowl and stir in the sugars. In another bowl, beat the eggs with the buttermilk, then pour onto the dry ingredients with the melted chocolate mixture.

4 Stir until everything is just combined, pour into the tin and bake for about 1 hour or until a skewer pushed into the cake comes out clean.

5 Leave to cool in the tin before turning out. When cold, split in half horizontally and sandwich with some of the frosting.

6 Spread more frosting over the top and sides. Decorate with sugarpaste or marzipan flowers and leaves and sugar sprinkles.

Serves 10
Prep time: 45 mins
Cook time: 45 mins

225 g/8 oz unsalted butter, softened
225 g/8 oz caster sugar
4 large eggs
225 g/8 oz plain flour
1 tsp vanilla essence

2 tsp baking powder
green food colouring

TO DECORATE
1 quantity of orange buttercream,
see page 12
coloured sugarpaste icing or
marzipan

Rainbow madeira with orange buttercream

1 Grease and line a 20 cm/8 in square cake tin. Preheat the oven to 180°C/350°F/Gas 4.

2 In a mixing bowl, beat the butter and sugar together until creamy. Beat in the eggs one at a time, adding a tablespoon of the flour with each egg. Stir in the vanilla, sieve in the rest of the flour and baking powder and fold in until evenly combined. Spoon half the mixture into a separate bowl and tint with a few drops of green food colouring.

3 Spoon alternate tablespoons of the mixture into the tin and bake for 45 minutes or until a skewer pushed into the centre comes out clean. Cool in the tin for 10 minutes before turning out onto a wire rack to cool completely and peeling off the paper.

4 Spread the buttercream over the cake and decorate with Dad's favourite tie, hat, socks and scarf. To make these, roll out the coloured icing or marzipan thinly on a board dusted with icing sugar. Cut out shapes in various colours with a sharp knife, dampen with a litte water and press together.

Serves 12
Prep time: 20 mins
Cook time: 55 mins–1 hour

250 g/9 oz unsalted butter, softened
250 g/9 oz caster sugar
4 large eggs
375 g/13 oz plain flour

175 g/6 oz raspberries, lightly crushed
1 tbsp baking powder
100 g/3 1/2 oz white chocolate, chopped
3 tbsp milk
icing sugar, to dust

Raspberry sponge ring

1 Grease and flour a 2.4 l/4 pt bundt tin or use a square or round cake tin with a similar capacity. Preheat the oven to 180°C/350°F/Gas 4.

2 In a mixing bowl, beat the butter and sugar together until creamy. Beat in the eggs one at a time, adding a tablespoon of the flour with each egg. Dust the raspberries with a little of the remaining flour. Sieve the rest of the flour into the bowl with the baking powder. Fold in with the white chocolate and raspberries. Finally stir in the milk.

3 Spoon the mixture into the tin, level and bake for 55 minutes to 1 hour or until a skewer pushed into the cake comes out clean. Cool in the tin for 10 minutes before turning out onto a wire rack to cool completely.

4 Serve the cake dusted with icing sugar.

TIP
Dusting the raspberries with a little flour before adding them to the cake mix prevents them from sinking during baking.

Serves 12
Prep time: 30 mins plus chilling
Cook time: 20 mins

4 large eggs
200 g/7 oz caster sugar
2 tbsp elderflower cordial
50 g/2 oz rice flour
115 g/4 oz plain flour
1½ tsp baking powder

FROSTING AND FILLING
300 g/11 oz strawberries
75 g/3 oz unsalted butter, softened
200 g/7 oz icing sugar
100 ml/3½ fl oz double cream
2 tbsp elderflower cordial

Strawberry and elderflower gâteau

1 Grease and base line two 20 cm/8 in sandwich tins,
4 cm/1½ in deep. Preheat the oven to 200°C/400°F/Gas 6.

2 In a bowl, beat the eggs, sugar and elderflower cordial until
creamy and pale-coloured. Sieve in the rice flour, plain flour
and baking powder. Gently fold in with a large metal spoon.

3 Divide the mixture between the tins, level and bake for
30 minutes or until golden and just firm. Cool in the tins
for 10 minutes before turning out onto a wire rack to cool
completely. Remove the papers.

4 For the frosting, mash 50 g/2 oz of the strawberries to a
purée. Beat the butter until smooth and sieve in the icing
sugar, beating well. Finally beat in the strawberry purée, then
chill until firm enough to spread over the top of one cake.

5 For the filling, whisk the cream with the elderflower cordial
until it holds its shape. Spread over the bottom cake layer.
Slice 4 or 5 strawberries and lay over the cream. Quarter the
rest and arrange over the frosting, then assemble the cake.

Serves 8
Prep time: 1 hour
Cook time: 40 mins

225 g/8 oz plain flour
1 tbsp baking powder
2 tbsp cocoa powder
200 g/7 oz light muscovado sugar
150 g/5 oz unsalted butter, melted
and cooled

3 large eggs
200 g/7 oz cooked pumpkin flesh,
mashed and cooled

TO DECORATE
1 quantity of orange buttercream,
see page 12
400 g/14 oz orange coloured
sugarpaste icing or marzipan and
small amounts of green, white and
black

Chocolate pumpkin cake

1 Grease and base line two 1.2 1/2 pt heatproof basins.
Preheat the oven to 180°C/350°F/Gas 4.

2 Sieve the flour, baking powder and cocoa powder into a
mixing bowl and stir in the sugar. In another bowl, beat
together the melted butter and eggs, then pour into the dry
ingredients, stirring until combined. Stir in the mashed
pumpkin.

3 Divide the mixture between the basins and spread level.
Bake for 40 minutes until a skewer pressed into the centre of
each cake comes out clean. Cool in the basins for 10 minutes
before turning out onto a wire rack to cool completely and
peeling off the papers.

4 To decorate, sandwich the two sponges together with some
of the buttercream and spread the rest over the outside. Roll
out the orange sugarpaste icing or marzipan and lift over the
cake, pressing it into place and marking 'pumpkin' ridges
down the sides with the handle of a wooden spoon. Cut
features from black and white icing or marzipan and a stalk
from green and fix in place with a dab of buttercream.

Serves 8
Prep time: 45 mins plus setting
Cook time: 20 mins

150 g/5 oz dark chocolate, chopped
5 large eggs, separated
150 g/5 oz caster sugar
2 tbsp cocoa powder

FILLING AND DECORATION
150 g/5 oz unsweetened chestnut purée
40 g/1½ oz icing sugar, plus extra to dust
150 ml/5 fl oz double cream
¾ quantity of dark chocolate icing, see page 13
edible gold leaf (optional)

Bûche de Noël

1 Grease and line a 33 x 23 cm/13 x 9 in Swiss roll tin. Preheat the oven to 180°C/350°F/Gas 4.

2 Melt the chocolate in a bowl over a pan of simmering water, stirring until smooth. In a large mixing bowl, whisk the egg yolks and sugar together until thick, creamy and pale-coloured. Sieve in the cocoa and fold in with the cooled, melted chocolate. In another bowl, whisk the egg whites until stiff. Stir 1 tablespoon into the chocolate mixture before gently folding in the rest.

3 Pour the mixture into the tin, spreading it to the corners, and bake for 20 minutes or until just firm to the touch.

4 Turn out onto a sheet of baking parchment and peel off the lining paper. Cover with a clean tea towel and leave to cool.

5 To fill and decorate, beat the chestnut purée and icing sugar together until smooth, then slowly whisk in the cream until light and fluffy. Spread over the roulade to within 1 cm/½ in of the edges and roll up from one long side. Pour the chocolate icing over, spreading with a palette knife to cover evenly and leave to set. Dust with icing sugar and, if wished, add small pieces of edible gold leaf.

3

fruits, nuts
& spices

Serves 10–12
Prep time: 30 mins
Cook time: 30 mins

250 g/9 oz plain flour
2 tsp baking powder
1 tsp ground cinnamon
200 g/7 oz light muscovado sugar
2 large eggs
200 ml/7 fl oz sunflower oil
2 small bananas, unpeeled weight
about 225 g/8 oz

150 g/5 oz grated carrot
50 g/2 oz sultanas
50 g/2 oz chopped walnuts

TO DECORATE
1 quantity of cream cheese frosting
with 1/2 tsp ground cinnamon added,
see page 13

coloured sugarpaste icing or
marzipan

Carrot and banana cake

1 Grease and line two 20 cm/8 in sandwich tins, 4 cm/1 1/2 in
deep. Preheat the oven to 180°C/350°F/Gas 4.

2 Sieve the flour, baking powder and cinnamon into a bowl
and stir in the sugar. Liquidize the eggs, oil and bananas
together until smooth and creamy, then fold into the dry
ingredients. Finally fold in the carrot, sultanas and walnuts.

3 Divide the mixture between the tins, level, and bake for
30 minutes or until a skewer inserted into the centre of each
cake comes out clean. Cool in the tins for 30 minutes before
turning out onto a wire rack to cool completely and peeling off
the papers.

4 To decorate, sandwich the cake layers with some of the
frosting and spread the rest on top. Arrange carrots and
bananas modelled from sugarpaste or
marzipan around the edge.

TIP
The riper the
bananas, the
sweeter and more
fragrant the finished
cake will be.

Serves 9
Prep time: 30 mins
Cook time: 45 mins

200 g/7 oz plain flour
2 tsp baking powder
150 g/5 oz unsalted butter, cut into small pieces
200 g/7oz light muscovado sugar
grated zest of 3 limes
2 large eggs

300 ml/10 fl oz buttermilk

TOPPING
25 g/1 oz unsalted butter, cut into small pieces
50 g/2 oz plain flour
5 tbsp light muscovado sugar
75 g/3 oz unsalted cashews, roughly chopped
juice of 3 limes

Lime drizzle cake with crunchy cashews

1 Grease and line a 19 cm/7 in square cake tin. Preheat the oven to 180°C/350°F/Gas 4.

2 Sieve the flour and baking powder into a mixing bowl, rub in the butter, then stir in the sugar. In another bowl, beat together the lime zest, eggs and buttermilk, pour into the flour mixture and whisk until evenly combined. Pour into the tin.

3 For the topping, rub the butter into the flour and stir in 1 tablespoon of the sugar and all of the cashews. Scatter over the top of the cake mixture.

4 Bake for 45 minutes or until a skewer pushed into the centre comes out clean. Stir together the rest of the sugar and the lime juice and spoon over the cake as soon as it comes out of the oven.

5 Leave to cool in the tin for 30 minutes before turning out onto a wire rack and removing the paper. Cut into squares and eat warm or cold.

Serves 8
Prep time: 30 mins
Cook time: 15–18 mins

4 large eggs, separated
150 g/5 oz caster sugar
3 tbsp plain flour
115 g/4 oz toasted hazelnuts, finely ground

FILLING

150 ml/5 fl oz double cream
2 tbsp apricot brandy or juice from the apricot can
caster sugar, to dust
411 g/14½ oz can of apricot halves in fruit juice, drained and chopped

Hazelnut and apricot roll

1 Grease and line a 33 x 23 cm/13 x 9 in Swiss roll tin. Preheat the oven to 180°C/350°F/Gas 4.

2 In a bowl, whisk the egg yolks and 125 g/4½ oz of the sugar until thick and pale-coloured. Sieve over the flour, scatter over the hazelnuts and fold in with a large metal spoon.

3 In another bowl, whisk the egg whites until stiff and gradually whisk in the remaining sugar until glossy. Stir a large spoonful into the egg yolk mixture, before carefully folding in the rest. Pour into the tin, level and bake for 15–18 minutes or until risen and just firm to the touch. Remove from the oven, cover with a damp tea cloth and leave to cool.

4 For the filling, whip the cream with the apricot brandy or juice until holding its shape. Sprinkle a sheet of baking parchment with caster sugar, turn out the sponge onto it and remove the lining paper. Spread the cream over the sponge to within 1 cm/½ in of the edges and add the chopped apricots.

5 Roll up the sponge starting from one short side. Transfer to a serving plate and chill until ready to serve. Sprinkle with extra sugar just before serving.

Serves 8–10
Prep time: 30 mins
Cook time: 45 mins

75 g/3 oz finely chopped fresh or tinned mango flesh
225 g/8 oz plain flour
175 g/6 oz unsalted butter, softened
200 g/7 oz golden caster sugar
3 large eggs

1 tbsp baking powder
1 tbsp finely chopped or grated, chilled, creamed coconut
2 tbsp milk

ICING AND DECORATION
3 passion fruit
150 g/5 oz icing sugar
fresh coconut shavings

Coconut and mango cake

1 Grease and flour a 1.6 l/2¾ pt kugelhopf tin or another tin with a similar capacity. Preheat the oven to 180°C/350°F/Gas 4.

2 Dust the chopped mango with a little of the flour. Put the butter, caster sugar, eggs, remaining flour and baking powder in a mixing bowl and add the grated coconut and milk. Whisk until the mixture is smooth and creamy. Finally stir in the mango.

3 Spoon into the tin, level and bake for 45 minutes or until a skewer pushed into the centre comes out clean. Cool in the tin for 5 minutes before turning out onto a wire rack to cool completely.

4 To make the icing, halve the passion fruit, scoop out the pulp and seeds of one fruit and add to the icing sugar. Scoop out the pulp and seeds from the other two into a small bowl and heat gently until the seeds separate from the pulp. Push through a sieve and stir the juice into the icing sugar until evenly mixed in.

5 Spread the icing over the top of the cake letting it run down the sides. Decorate with shavings of fresh coconut.

Serves 8–10

Prep time: 30 mins plus infusing and setting

Cook time: 45 mins

2 tbsp milk

1 tsp fresh or dried lavender flowers (if fresh, use unsprayed flowers or cook's lavender from specialist suppliers)

175 g/6 oz unsalted butter, softened

175 g/6 oz caster sugar

grated zest of 1 small lemon

3 large eggs

225 g/8 oz plain flour

2 tsp baking powder

TO DECORATE

1 quantity of lemon glacé icing, see page 12

lavender sprigs (optional)

Lavender sponge with lemon glacé icing

1 Put the milk in a small bowl, add the lavender flowers and heat gently in the microwave for 15 seconds or until the milk is hot. Remove and set aside to infuse for 30 minutes.

2 Grease and flour a 1.5 l/2½ pt bundt or ring tin. Preheat the oven to 180°C/350°F/Gas 4.

3 In a mixing bowl, beat together the butter, sugar and lemon zest until creamy. Beat in the eggs one at a time, adding a tablespoon of the flour with each egg, then sieve in the rest of the flour and baking powder and fold in. Stir in the lavender and its soaking milk to soften the mixture.

4 Spoon into the tin, level and bake for 45 minutes or until a skewer inserted into the cake comes out clean. Cool in the tin for 10 minutes, before turning out onto a wire rack to cool completely.

5 Place the cake on a serving plate and spoon or pipe the icing over. Decorate with lavender sprigs, if using, and leave to set.

Serves 10
Prep time: 20 mins
Cook time: 50 mins

115 g/4 oz honey
150 g/5 oz dark muscovado sugar
1 tsp ground anise seed
1 tsp ground ginger

1 tsp ground cinnamon
1 tsp finely grated orange or lemon zest
100 ml/3½ fl oz water
250 g/9 oz plain flour
2 tsp baking powder
1 large egg, beaten
75 g/3 oz chopped pecans

Pecan pain d'épice

1 Grease and line a 1.2 1/2 pt loaf tin. Preheat the oven to 170°C/325°F/Gas 3.

2 Put the honey, sugar, ground spices, orange or lemon zest and water in a pan and heat gently until the honey and sugar melt, stirring regularly with a wooden spoon.

3 Sieve the flour and baking powder together and add to the melted mixture with the egg and pecans. Stir until evenly combined.

4 Spoon the mixture into the tin and bake for 50 minutes or until a skewer pushed into the centre comes out clean. Leave to cool in the tin for 30 minutes before turning out onto a wire rack and removing the paper. Eat warm or cold. The cake has quite a dry texture, so is also good spread with butter.

TIP
Ground anise seed can be found in Middle Eastern stores but you could substitute 1 tsp fenugreek or caraway seeds.

Serves 8
Prep time: 30 mins
Cook time: 45 mins

150 g/5 oz unsalted butter, softened
200 g/7 oz caster sugar
finely grated zest of 1 orange and
2 lemons
4 large eggs
150 g/5 oz plain flour
2 tsp baking powder
115 g/4 oz ground almonds

SPICED SYRUP AND DECORATION
juice of 1 orange and 2 lemons
65 g/2½ oz caster sugar
1 tsp ground cinnamon
½ tsp ground mixed spice
1 orange, peeled and sliced
2 tbsp chopped pistachios
2 tbsp orange jelly marmalade,
optional (see method)

Citrus syrup cake

1 Grease and line a 20 cm/8 in round cake tin. Preheat the oven to 170°C/325°F/Gas 3.

2 Cream the butter and sugar together with the citrus zests. Beat in the eggs one at a time, adding a tablespoon of the flour with each egg. Sieve in the rest of the flour and baking powder and fold in with the ground almonds.

3 Spoon into the tin, level and bake for 45 minutes or until a skewer pushed into the centre comes out clean.

4 To make the syrup, put the citrus juices and sugar in a small pan and add the spices. Heat gently until the sugar has dissolved, then simmer for 2 minutes. Spoon over the cake as soon as it comes out of the oven and leave to cool in the tin.

5 Turn the cake out, remove the paper and decorate with orange segments and chopped pistachios. If not serving immediately, brush the segments with the warmed jelly marmalade to prevent them from drying out.

Serves 8–10
Prep time: 20 mins
Cook time: 45 mins

4 sprigs of soft fresh rosemary, each
about 7.5 cm/3 in long
175 g/6 oz unsalted butter, softened

175 g/6 oz caster sugar
finely grated zest of 1 small orange
3 large eggs
225 g/8 oz plain flour
2 tsp baking powder
icing sugar, to dust

Orange and rosemary madeira cake

1 Grease and flour a 1.5 l/2½ pt bundt tin. Preheat the oven to 180°C/350°F/Gas 4.

2 Strip the rosemary leaves from their stalks and chop very finely. In a mixing bowl, beat the butter until creamy, then gradually beat in the sugar, orange zest and rosemary.

3 Beat in the eggs one at a time, adding a tablespoon of the flour with each egg. Sieve in the rest of the flour and baking powder and fold in.

4 Spoon the mixture into the tin, level and bake for 45 minutes or until a skewer pushed into the centre comes out clean. Leave to cool in the tin for 10 minutes before turning out onto a wire rack to cool completely.

5 Serve dusted with icing sugar.

TIP
Be sure to use rosemary leaves that are young, green and tender as older ones will be tough and dry.

Serves 8

Prep time: 20 mins

Cook time: 40 mins

4 medium-sized ripe but firm peaches (unprepared weight approx. 350 g/12 oz)

400 g/14 oz plain flour

4 large eggs

250 g/9 oz golden caster sugar

finely grated zest of 1 lemon

1 tsp baking powder

1 tsp ground cinnamon

150 g/5 oz unsalted butter, melted and cooled

4 tbsp apricot jam

3 amaretti biscuits, crushed

Spicy peach and lemon torte

1 Grease and flour a 1.8 l/3 pt ring tin. Preheat the oven to 180°C/350°F/Gas 4.

2 Put 2 of the peaches in a heatproof bowl, pour over boiling water to cover and leave for 1 minute. Drain and, when cool enough to handle, halve the fruit, remove the stones and strip off the skins. Chop and dust with a little of the flour.

3 Whisk the eggs, caster sugar and lemon zest together in a mixing bowl until thick and pale-coloured. Sieve in the rest of the flour, baking powder and cinnamon, drizzle the melted butter around the edge of the bowl and gently fold all the ingredients together using a large metal spoon until combined.

4 Spoon half the mixture into the tin and scatter the chopped peaches on top. Spoon over the rest of the mixture and level. Bake for 40 minutes or until a skewer pushed into the cake comes out clean. Leave to cool in the tin for 10 minutes before turning out onto a wire rack to cool completely.

5 Warm the apricot jam and brush half over the top of the cake. Peel the remaining peaches, remove the stones and cut into slices. Arrange over the cake, brush with the remaining jam and sprinkle with the crushed amaretti.

4

free from...

Serves 9

Prep time: 30 mins

Cook time: 40–45 mins plus time for mashed potatoes

200 g/7 oz unsalted butter, softened
200 g/7 oz caster sugar
finely grated zest of 3 lemons
4 large eggs
175 g/6 oz rice flour

225 g/8 oz cooked potatoes, mashed and cooled
2 tsp gluten-free baking powder
2 tbsp poppy seeds

TO DECORATE
1 quantity of lemon glacé icing, see page 12
sugar sprinkles

Lemon and poppy seed rice cake

1 Grease and line a 19 cm/7 in square cake tin. Preheat the oven to 180°C/350°F/Gas 4.

2 Beat the butter, sugar and lemon zest together until creamy. Beat in the eggs one at a time, adding a tablespoon of the rice flour with each egg. Stir in the rest of the rice flour, the mashed potatoes, baking powder and poppy seeds.

3 Spoon into the tin, level and bake for 40–45 minutes or until a skewer pushed into the centre comes out clean. Cool in the tin for 10 minutes before turning out onto a wire rack to cool completely.

4 To decorate, drizzle or spread the icing over the cake and scatter with sugar sprinkles.

TIP
The same quantity of ground almonds or polenta could replace the rice flour.

Serves 8
Prep time: 30 mins
Cook time: 40 mins

200 g/7 oz dark chocolate, chopped
115 g/4 oz unsalted butter, cut into
small pieces

4 large eggs, separated
150 g/5 oz caster sugar
2 tbsp dark rum or milk
75 g/3 oz fine polenta
icing sugar, to dust

Chocolate polenta cake

1 Grease and line a 20 cm/8 in round cake tin. Preheat the oven to 180°C/350°F/Gas 4.

2 Put the chocolate and butter in a pan and heat gently until melted.

3 In a mixing bowl, beat the egg yolks with half the sugar until pale and thick. Whisk in 1 tablespoon of the rum or milk, then fold in the melted chocolate mixture.

4 In another bowl, whisk the egg whites until standing in soft peaks. Gradually whisk in the remaining sugar until thick and shiny. Add the rest of the rum or milk and the polenta to the egg yolk mixture and fold in until combined.

5 Stir in 1 tablespoon of the whisked whites, then carefully fold in the remainder using a large metal spoon. Pour into the tin, level and bake for about 40 minutes or until a skewer pushed into the centre comes out clean.

6 Remove from the oven and cool in the tin for 15 minutes before turning out onto a serving plate to cool completely. Remove the paper. Serve dusted with icing sugar.

TIP
As the cake is quite fragile, it's best to let it cool in the tin for about 15 minutes, then turn it out directly onto a serving plate.

Serves 8

Prep time: 20 mins

Cook time: 40 mins plus cooking time for sweet potatoes

175 g/6 oz unsalted butter, softened
175 g/6 oz caster sugar
4 large eggs
175 g/6 oz ground almonds

225 g/8 oz steamed sweet potatoes (about 2 medium), mashed and cooled
finely grated zest of 1 large orange
2 tsp gluten-free baking powder

DRIZZLE
6 tbsp icing sugar
1 tbsp orange juice
fine shreds of orange zest

Sweet potato and orange drizzle cake

1 Grease and line a 20 cm/8 in round cake tin. Preheat the oven to 180°C/350°F/Gas 4.

2 Beat the butter and sugar in a mixing bowl until creamy. Beat in the eggs one at a time, adding a tablespoon of the ground almonds with each egg. Stir in the remaining almonds, sweet potato mash, orange zest and baking powder.

3 Spoon into the tin, level and bake for 40 minutes or until a skewer inserted into the centre comes out clean.

4 Cool in the tin for 15 minutes before turning out onto a wire rack to cool completely and peeling off the paper.

5 Stir the orange juice into the icing sugar and drizzle over the cake. Decorate with the orange zest.

TIP
Gluten-free baking powder is available from larger supermarkets, check labels of containers before buying.

Serves 8
Prep time: 25 mins
Cook time: 40–45 mins

175 g/6 oz unsalted butter, softened
175 g/6 oz caster sugar
grated zest and juice of 1 orange
3 small, ripe bananas, about
350 g/12 oz unpeeled weight
115 g/4 oz redcurrants or
lingonberries

275 g/10 oz plain flour
2 tsp baking powder
1/2 tsp bicarbonate of soda
115 ml/4 fl oz milk

TO DECORATE
150 g/5 oz unsalted butter, softened
115 ml/4 fl oz full-fat soured cream
250 g/9 oz icing sugar, sieved
small sprigs of redcurrants

Banana, orange and redcurrant ring

1 Grease and flour a 1.8 l/3 pt ring tin. Preheat the oven to 180°C/350°F/Gas 4.

2 In a bowl, beat the butter and sugar together until creamy, then stir in the orange zest. Mash the bananas with the orange juice and stir in until evenly mixed. Dust the redcurrants or lingonberries with a little of the flour. Sieve the rest of the flour, baking powder and bicarbonate of soda into the banana mixture and stir in. Finally add the milk and redcurrants or lingonberries and mix in.

3 Spoon into the tin and bake for 40–45 minutes or until a skewer pushed into the cake comes out clean. Note, this egg-free cake has a denser texture than normal. Cool in the tin for 15 minutes, then turn out onto a wire rack to cool completely.

4 To decorate, beat the butter until creamy and smooth. Mix together the soured cream and icing sugar, then beat into the butter. Chill until thick enough to spread over the ring. Arrange small sprigs of redcurrants or lingonberries on top.

Serves 12

Prep time: 40 mins

Cook time: 30 mins

2 large eggs

150 ml/5 fl oz sunflower oil

175 g/6 oz apricots halves, fresh or tinned in juice, chopped

275 g/10 oz plain flour

1 tbsp baking powder

225 g/8 oz grated carrots

200 ml/7 fl oz unsweetened orange juice

FROSTING

50 g/2oz unsalted butter, softened

175 g/6 oz full-fat cream cheese

2 tsp unsweetened orange juice

extra apricot halves, fresh or tinned in juice, sliced

2 tbsp chopped pistachios

sugar-free sweetener (optional)

sugar-free

Apricot bars with cream cheese

1 Grease and line a 19 x 27.5 cm/7 x 11 in tin – a small roasting tin works well. Preheat the oven to 180°C/350°F/Gas 4.

2 Put the eggs in a mixing bowl and slowly whisk in the oil in a thin stream so it is incorporated smoothly into the eggs and the mixture is creamy and pale-coloured. Dust the apricots with a little of the flour.

3 Sieve the remaining flour and baking powder into the bowl and fold in with the carrots, apricots and orange juice.

4 Spoon into the tin and bake for 30 minutes or until a skewer pushed into the centre comes out clean. Cool in the tin for 10 minutes before turning out onto a wire rack to cool and peeling off the paper.

5 For the frosting, whisk together the butter, cream cheese and orange juice until smooth. Add a little sugar-free sweetener, if desired. Spread over the top of the cake and cut into 12 bars. Decorate each one with sliced apricots and chopped pistachios.

Serves 8

Prep time: 30 mins

Cook time: 30 mins

3 large eggs

150 g/5 oz golden caster sugar

90 g/3¹/₂ oz plain flour

1 tsp ground ginger

TO DECORATE

8 tbsp apricot jam

1 tbsp lemon juice

5 slices of pineapple, fresh or tinned in fruit juice, chopped

50 g/2 oz raspberries

Ginger genoese with pineapple

1 Grease and line a 23 cm/9 in spring-clip or round cake tin. Preheat the oven to 180°C/350°F/Gas 4.

2 Put the eggs and sugar in a mixing bowl, stand the bowl over a pan of simmering water, without letting the bottom of the bowl touch the water, and whisk for about 5 minutes or until pale and mousse-like. Remove the bowl to the work surface and continue whisking until the base of it feels cool.

3 Sieve in the flour and ginger, then fold in gently with a large metal spoon. Pour into the tin, tap the tin lightly on the work surface to release any air bubbles and bake for 30 minutes or until the cake is just shrinking from the sides of the tin and springs back when pressed.

4 Cool in the tin for 10 minutes before turning out onto a wire rack to cool completely. Remove the paper.

5 To decorate, heat the jam with the lemon juice, then sieve to remove any large pieces of fruit. Brush the top of the cake with half the jam and arrange the chopped pineapple and raspberries on top. Brush with the rest of the jam.

Serves 8
Prep time: 30 mins
Cook time: 50 mins

75 g/3 oz blueberries
115 g/4 oz plain flour
175 g/6 oz ground almonds
110 g/3½ oz caster sugar
3 large eggs, beaten
75 ml/3 fl oz sunflower oil

1½ tsp baking powder
5 tbsp coconut milk

ICING AND DECORATION
50 g/2 oz icing sugar
about 1 tbsp coconut milk
2 tbsp desiccated coconut, lightly toasted
extra blueberries

Blueberry and coconut cake

1 Grease and line a 1.2 1/2 pt loaf tin. Preheat the oven to 180°C/350°F/Gas 4.

2 Dust the blueberries with a little of the flour. Put the almonds, sugar, eggs, oil, baking powder, coconut milk and the remaining flour in a large mixing bowl and whisk or beat together until smooth. Stir in the blueberries.

3 Spoon the mixture into the tin and bake for 50 minutes or until a skewer pushed into the centre comes out clean. Cool in the tin for 10 minutes before turning out onto a wire rack to cool completely. Remove the paper.

4 To decorate, stir the icing sugar and enough coconut milk together to make a smooth, runny icing and drizzle over the cake. Top with toasted desiccated coconut and extra blueberries.

TIP
Instead of blueberries, the cake could be made with redcurrants, blackcurrants or lingonberries.

Recipe index